Yoruba Mythology: The Gods and Goddesses of Yorubaland

Copyright © 2017 by Nzinga-Christina Reid

Written by Nzinga-Christina Reid

Illustrated by Goldest Karat Art

All rights reserved. No part of this book may be used or reproduced in any manner whatsoever without the prior written permission of the author.

Black Diaries Publishing
1128 Lenox Rd
Suite 2R
Brooklyn, NY 11212

For more information, visit us online at
www.blackdiaries.org

**In loving memory of Patrick Baker
who let me know my dreams are valid.**

Yoruba Mythology:
The Gods and Goddesses of Yorubaland

Yoruba mythology, a collection of cultural and religious myths about the ancient gods and goddesses of West Africa, is an often studied subject, yet much is still unknown. This book explores (and encourages YOU to explore) the mythic nature of their individual characters.

African spirits, or Orishas of the Yoruba people, are said to number more than 400 deities. The Yoruba people are mostly found in western Nigeria as well as in parts of Benin, specifically in an area called Yorubaland.

Similar to the gods and goddesses of Greek mythology, each Orisha usually protects and assists humankind in some manner. Aborisha, or people of the Yoruba faith, believe that the Supreme God Olorun has given everything on Earth a spiritual life force, an energy known as Ase (or àṣẹ, ashe) meaning the 'power to make things happen' or produce change. Ase is also a globally exchanged greeting among many communities of the African Diaspora. Many think the power of Ase is active within us all.

Yoruba mythology spread through the Transatlantic Slave Trade. Those Africans captured and forced into slavery brought their traditions into the New World after leaving the continent through Gberefu Island—known as 'The Point Of No Return'— in Lagos, Nigeria. They held on to their teachings and continued in their practices. The Yoruba traditions today are found in various forms throughout the Caribbean, South America (mostly Brazil), and North America.

As the Orisha stories were passed down orally through the centuries, there evolved many variations of the characters, their name spellings, and their relationships to one another. This book presents one variation of the better-known gods and goddess, and their personalities.

I am the tri-part Supreme God of the universe, called Olodumare, the ultimate creator, Olofi the messenger between heaven and Earth, and Olorun the god of heaven and the sun. Put us all together, see we make one.

Greetings, I am Obatala the sky god and the father of all humanity. My name combines Oba—translated to powerful king—and Tala, which means spilled, extension, expansion. As the second son of the Supreme God Olorun, find me high in the sky dressed in all white. So some know me as the White Cloth God.

Peace unto you! I am Yemaya, goddess of the ocean, motherhood, and mother to many Orishas. I first lived at the Ogun River, as the goddess there. When Europeans came and kidnapped my people, I then traveled with them onto slave ships comforting them during their forced migration. Now I am known as Mother Ocean, with dominance over the surface of the seas.

Wise. Knowledgeable. Seer of the future. I am Orunmila. The spirit of wisdom, prophecy, and the divinity of destiny are what I possess. I am the first son of the Supreme God Olorun.

I, Eshu, am a trickster, unpredictable, sly, and a lover of pranks. I speak all the languages of the world so I serve as a messenger between the humans and the gods.

Ase. I am Ogun, the warrior god of iron and metal.
I will clear away all obstacles in your path with my iron sword in hand.

They call me Osoosi, the forest god of hunting and justice. Known for my high morals and ethics, as well as being a skilled tracker, I can help you navigate the shortest path to your spiritual goals.

Hello there. Aganju is my name, god of volcanoes and the wilderness.
I am also the god of untamed lands, from deserts to mountains.
I steer you to the safe passages to guide your travels.

Shango is who I am. God of thunder, lightning, justice, and dance. Hear me play rhythms on my storm clouds, banging the bata double-headed drums to summon the storms. People hear my beat, and move their feet in joyous dance. I am husband to Oba, Oya and, my favorite, Oshun.

Great Rising. I am the dark warrior goddess Oya, called the goddess of the storm and wind. I make lightning and tornadoes by whirling my skirt in a dance.
Cross my path...if you dare.

I, Egungun-oya, daughter of Oya, am the goddess of foretelling the future and fate.
Some call me the Mother of the Dead. I peek into your future in the land of the living,
and I guide our ancestors in the afterlife.

Good Day from Oba, goddess of the Oba River.
I am the domestic goddess of the home and the daughter of Yemaya.
I am the first, yet distant, wife of Shango and have a fierce rivalry with Oshun.

Blessings Kings and Queens. I am Oshun, goddess of the river, love, and fertility. I bring pleasure to followers, but indescribable pain and destruction to those who anger me. I reign as Shango's principle wife.

We are Ibeji, the sacred twins; one soul in two bodies, male and female.
Shango and Oshun are our parents. We are full of joy, mischief, abundance, and childish glee.
We protect twins everywhere.

Peace and blessings from Osanyin, the spirit of the forest plants and healing.
As the keeper of herbs with magical properties, I know their secrets, making me a natural healer.
Bring me your sick.

Babalu-Aye is who I be, the god who spreads illness and disease—it doesn't bother me.
Yet I am also the spirit that cures sicknesses.
Extremely powerful and feared, yet respected by all.

Do you see me in the sky? I am the serpent and the rainbow; however, you can call me Osumare. I represent transformation, movement, and the union between heaven and Earth. Babalu-Aye is my brother.

Look at the bottom of the sea, that's where you'll find me. I am the sea goddess Olokun.
My name means owner (Olo) of oceans (Kun). That's me, the ruler of the deep dark sea.
I possess unfathomable wisdom, wealth, and so many secrets it's hard to believe.

I am the father of the land. I am Oko, god of agriculture, farming, and the harvest.
I live on a farm, helping the soil produce an abundant harvest of vegetables and fruit.
I also judge disputes amongst the Orishas.

Good Day to you. I am Erinle, god of hunting and the wilderness.
I also produce herbs for healing ailments.
I am praised for being an Orisha of wealth and prosperity.